The official
ASTON VILLA
FOOTBALL CLUB ANNUAL
2016

AVFC

PREPARED

Compiled by Rob Bishop and Tricia Mills

A Grange Publication

© 2015. Published by Grange Communications Ltd., Edinburgh, under licence from Aston Villa Football Club. Printed in the EU.

Special thanks to Gayner Monkton and Lorna McCelland

Photographs © Neville Williams and Getty Images

ISBN 978-1-910199-40-4

Club Honours

EUROPEAN CUP WINNERS: 1981-82
QUARTER-FINALISTS: 1982-83

EUROPEAN SUPER CUP WINNERS: 1982-83

WORLD CLUBS CHAMPIONSHIP RUNNERS-UP: 1982

INTERTOTO CUP WINNERS: 2001

FOOTBALL LEAGUE
CHAMPIONS: 1893-94, 1895-96, 1896-97, 1898-99, 1899-1900, 1909-10, 1980-81
RUNNERS-UP: 1888-89, 1902-03, 1907-08, 1910-11, 1912-13, 1913-14, 1930-31, 1932-33, 1989-90

PREMIER LEAGUE RUNNERS-UP: 1992-93

DIVISION TWO CHAMPIONS: 1937-38, 1959-60

DIVISION THREE CHAMPIONS: 1971-72

FA CUP
WINNERS: 1887, 1895, 1897, 1905, 1913, 1920, 1957
RUNNERS-UP: 1892, 1924, 2000, 2015

LEAGUE CUP
WINNERS: 1961, 1975, 1977, 1994, 1996
RUNNERS-UP: 1963, 1971, 2010

FA YOUTH CUP WINNERS: 1972, 1980, 2002
RUNNERS-UP: 2004, 2010

NEXTGEN SERIES WINNERS: 2013

Contents

From Viola to Villa

The colours are similar, but Micah Richards was more than happy to swap the purple of the Viola for the claret and blue of Villa.

The 27-year-old defender joined us from Manchester City, although he spent last season on loan with Italian club Fiorentina, who play in violet.

Micah's year in Florence wasn't as productive as he would have liked – he played just 10 Serie A matches plus seven Europa League ties and two Italian Cup games. But there will be no complaints if his time at Villa Park is as successful as his 10 years at the City of Manchester Stadium.

He made a total of 245 appearances, winning a Premier League medal and also helping City to FA Cup and League Cup glory.

On top of the world

Jordan Ayew couldn't disguise his delight when he became a Villa player. On the day he signed from French club Lorient, the 24-year-old striker declared: "I am the happiest man in the world – this is one of my greatest days in football.

"My dream was to play for a big team in England, and Aston Villa are one of the greats in English football. The Premier League is the biggest in the world so when the opportunity came I didn't think twice."

Ayew started his senior career with his home city club Marseille and played more than 130 games for them. Last season he moved to Lorient – and his 12 league goals helped them to retain Ligue 1 status.

Powers of persuasion...

A conversation with Tim Sherwood persuaded Idrissa Gana that he should head for the West Midlands rather than pursue his career in the south of France.

The highly-rated defensive midfielder was wanted by Marseille but rejected that option after meeting Villa's manager.

"The coach and I got on well straight away," said the Senegal international, who established himself as a key player with Lille before his transfer to Villa Park.

"I saw the vision of how he wants us to play and where he planned to use me – he had watched a lot of my games and that gave me confidence. He told me some very nice things and that persuaded me to take the decision to come here."

NICE one, Jordan

Young football supporters love meeting their heroes face to face and Jordan Amavi is only too happy to oblige.

The 21-year-old French left-back arrived at Villa Park from Nice with a message that he has no problem in signing autographs or posing for photos with the fans.

"I want to make a big bond with the supporters," he said. "I want them to be proud of me – I want them to see that I am good for the team.

"Supporters are vital. I am the sort of person who has his photo taken with them or signs autographs, I take that seriously. It's important because the fans mean so much to the club."

I'm my own man

It's always flattering to be compared to a top-class performer, so Jordan Veretout was delighted when people started likening his style to that of Arsenal star Aaron Ramsey.

But the French midfielder is equally determined to become a star in his own right after arriving from Nantes.

"I am very flattered that people think I remind them of Aaron because he is a very good player," he said. "But at the same time I am my own player and play my own game. I want to develop here at Aston Villa.

"I like to be creative, making goals for my team-mates – and I also love scoring."

Tower of strength

Rudy Gestede needed less than a quarter of an hour to establish himself as a big favourite with the claret-and-blue faithful.

The French marksman went on as a 59th-minute substitute in Villa's opening game of the season at Bournemouth – and in the 72nd minute he headed the winning goal.

Not only that, he became the first Villa sub to score on the opening day of the season.

Tall strikers have invariably been popular with Villa supporters, and Rudy, who is 6ft 4in, has vowed to follow in the footsteps of players like Peter Crouch and John Carew.

After signing from Championship club Blackburn Rovers, the French marksman revealed: "Many strikers have been successful here and I hope to follow the same path. I know the No 9-style of player has been popular with the fans and hopefully I will have a similar impact."

THE NEW >> BOYS

Hola Jose!

It's not always easy for foreign players to make themselves understood when they join a new club. But that was no problem for Jose Angel Crespo.

When the 28-year-old Spanish defender checked in at Villa's Bodymoor Heath training ground, the first person to interview him was fellow Spaniard Carles Gil! The duo happily agreed to face the AVTV HD cameras, with Carles taking charge of the microphone to provide a novel piece of footage for the club's official television channel.

The not-so new boy...

Scott Sinclair needed no introduction to his team-mates when he became a Villa player – he had been playing alongside them for three months!

The midfielder arrived at Villa Park during the January transfer window on loan from Manchester City, and the move became permanent in May after the boys in claret and blue had secured Premier League safety.

That was great news for Sinclair, who has spent most of his career as a football nomad with a host of different clubs. Now he wants to make an impact at Villa player after signing a four-year contract.

Just like Messi...

Adama Traore didn't have to think twice when he was asked about the biggest influence on his career.

The young winger learned his trade with Barcelona and even played a few games for the first team of the Spanish giants.

So it was no surprise to learn that the brilliant Lionel Messi is his role model – and not just because Messi is regarded as the best player in the world.

"All the academy players at Barcelona follow Messi's example," said Traore. "From him, you can see how to be humble and work hard. Talent alone is not enough. You have to use it in the right way."

Canary keepers

Mark Bunn became the second goalkeeper to join Villa from Norwich City in the space of two years when he signed in July. He followed in the footsteps of Jed Steer, who made the move from Carrow Road to Villa Park in July 2013.

The 30-year-old Londoner began his career with Northampton and also played for Blackburn Rovers, plus loan spells with Leicester City and Sheffield United before joining Norwich in 2012. He played 31 games for the Canaries.

A Villa victory?

It's the big match – but can you help Villa to victory? All you need is a dice, two counters and a friend to provide the opposition. First one to the top gets three points!

FULL-TIME
who won?

| 28 | 27 | 26 | 25 |

| 20 | 21 | **RED CARD BACK TO START!** 22 | 23 | 24 **GREAT VOLLEY MOVE ON 3** |

| **DIVING HEADER MOVE ON 4** 19 | 18 | **OWN GOAL GO BACK 1** 17 | 16 | 15 **HALF-TIME MISS A TURN** |

| **PENALTY! MOVE ON 3** 10 | 11 | 12 **YELLOW CARD GO BACK 1** | 13 | **SUBSTITUTION MOVE ON 2** 14 |

| 9 | 8 **PLAYER INJURED GO BACK 3** | **IT'S A CORNER MOVE ON 2** 7 | 6 | 5 |

| **KICK OFF!** | 1 | **EARLY PRESSURE MOVE ON 2** 2 | 3 | 4 |

MORE THAN 90 MINUTES...

Matchday at Villa Park is about much more than 90 minutes of action on the pitch.
The match is obviously the main event but for many people, watching Villa is a day out with family or friends, and the air of anticipation is almost as exciting as the game itself – as these photos clearly illustrate.

Will we win today, Dad?

Watching the players arrive

Stars of Trinity Road

What's in the programme?

GOALKEEPER

BRAD GUZAN

Born: CHICAGO, USA, 09.09.1984
Signed: AUGUST 2008
Previous club: CHIVAS USA
Debut: QPR (h) 24.09.2008

GOALKEEPER

MARK BUNN

Born: LONDON, 16.11.1984
Signed: JULY 2015
Previous club: NORWICH CITY
Debut: NOTTS COUNTY (h) 25.08.2015

VILLANS
ON THE CARDS

GOALKEEPER
JED STEER

Born: NORWICH, 23.09.1992
Signed: JULY 2013
Previous club: NORWICH CITY
Debut: ROTHERHAM UNITED (h) 28.08.2013

LEFT-BACK
JOE BENNETT

Born: RICHDALE, 28.03.1990
Signed: AUGUST 2012
Previous club: MIDDLESBROUGH
Debut: SOUTHAMPTON (a) 22.09.2012

RIGHT-BACK
ALAN HUTTON

Born: GLASGOW, 30.11.1984
Signed: AUGUST 2011
Previous club: TOTTENHAM HOTSPUR
Debut: EVERTON (a) 10.09.2011

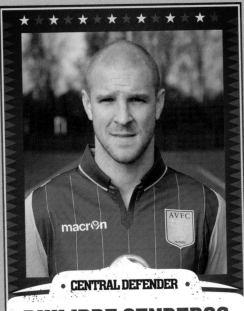

CENTRAL DEFENDER
PHILIPPE SENDEROS

Born: GENEVA, SWITZERLAND, 14.02.1985
Signed: JULY 2014
Previous club: VALENCIA
Debut: STOKE CITY (a) 16.08.2014

CENTRE-BACK

CIARAN CLARK

Born: HARROW, 26.09.1989
Signed: ACADEMY GRADUATE
Debut: FULHAM (h) 30.08.2009

CENTRE-BACK

NATHAN BAKER

Born: WORCESTER, 23.04.1991
Signed: ACADEMY GRADUATE
Debut: WIGAN ATHLETIC (a)
25.01.2011

MIDFIELDER

LEANDRO BACUNA

Born: GRONINGEN, NETHERLANDS
21.08.1991
Signed: JUNE 2013
Previous club: GRONINGEN
Debut: ARSENAL (a) 18.08.2013

MIDFIELDER

ASHLEY WESTWOOD

Born: NANTWICH, 01.04.1990
Signed: AUGUST 2012
Previous club: CREWE ALEXANDRA
Debut: SWANSEA CITY (h)
15.09.2012

MIDFIELDER

GARY GARDNER

Born: SOLIHUILL, 29.06.1992
Signed: ACADEMY GRADUATE
Debut: CHELSEA (a) 31.12.2011

MIDFIELDER

CHARLES N'ZOGBIA

Born: HARFLEUR, FRANCE,
28.05.1986
Signed: JULY 2011
Previous club: WIGAN ATHLETIC
Debut: FULHAM (a) 13.08.2011

STRIKER

GABBY AGBONLAHOR

Born: BIRMINGHAM, 13.10.1986
Signed: ACADEMY GRADUATE
Debut: EVERTON (a) 18.03.2006

CENTRE-BACK

JORES OKORE

Born: ABIDJAN, IVORY COAST,
11.08.1992
Signed: JUNE 2013
Previous club: NORDSJAELLAND

MIDFIELDER
JOE COLE
Born: LONDON, 08.11.1981
Signed: JUNE 2014
Previous club: WEST HAM
DébUT: LEYTON ORIENT (h) 27.08.2014

• LEFT BACK/MIDFIELD •
KIERAN RICHARDSON
Born: LONDON 21.10.1984
Signed: JULY 2014
Previous club: FULHAM
Debut: STOKE CITY (a) 16.08.2014

STRIKER
LIBOR KOZAK
Born: OPAVA, CZECH REPUBLIC, 30.05.1989
Signed: SEPTEMBER 2013
Previous club: LAZIO
Debut: NEWCASTLE UNITED (h)
14.09.2013

MIDFIELDER
JACK GREALISH
Born: BIRMINGHAM, 10.09.1995
Signed: ACADEMY GRADUATE
Debut: MANCHESTER CITY (a)
07.05.2014

MIDFIELDER
CARLOS SANCHEZ

Born: QUIBDO, COLOMBIA 06.02.1986
Signed: AUGUST 2014
Previous club: ELCHE
Debut: NEWCASTLE UNITED (h)
23.08.2014

MIDFIELDER
CARLES GIL

Born: VALENCIA, SPAIN, 22.11.1992
Signed: JANUARY 2015
Previous club: VALENCIA
Debut: LIVERPOOL (h) 17.01.2015

DEFENDER
JOLEON LESCOTT

Born: BIRMINGHAM, 16.08.1982
Signed: SEPTEMBER 2015
Previous club: WEST BROMWICH
ALBION

MIDFIELDER
SCOTT SINCLAIR

Born: BATH, 26.03.1989
Signed: JANUARY 2015 (loan)
Previous club: MANCHESTER CITY
Debut: ARSENAL (a) 01.02.2015

DEFENDER

MICAH RICHARDS

Born: BIRMINGHAM, 24.06.1988
Signed: JUNE 2015
Previous club: MANCHESTER CITY
Debut: BOURNEMOUTH (A) 08.08.2015

STRIKER

JORDAN AYEW

Born: MARSEILLE, FRANCE, 11.09.1991
Signed: JULY 2015
Previous club: LORIENT
Debut: BOURNEMOUTH (A) 08.08.2015

MIDFIELDER

IDRISSA GANA

Born: DAKAR, SENEGAL, 26.09.1989
Signed: JULY 2015
Previous club: LILLE OSC
Debut: BOURNEMOUTH (A) 08.08.2015

DEFENDER

JORDAN AMAVI

Born: TOULON, FRANCE 09.03.1994
Signed: JULY 2015
Previous club: NICE
Debut: BOURNEMOUTH (A) 08.08.2015

DEFENDER

JOSE ANGEL CRESPO

Born: LORA DEL RIO, SPAIN, 09.02.1987
Signed: JULY 2015
Previous club: CORDOBA

MIDFIELDER

ADAMA TRAORE

Born: L'HOSPITALET DE LLOBREGAT,
SPAIN, 25.01.1996
Signed: AUGUST 2015
Previous club: BARCELONA
Debut: CRYSTAL PALACE (a) 22.08.2015

STRIKER

RUDY GESTEDE

Born: ESSEY-LES-NANCY, FRANCE,
10.10.1988
Signed: JULY 2015
Previous club: BLACKBURN ROVERS
Debut: BOURNEMOUTH (A) 08.08.2015

MIDFIELDER

JORDAN VERETOUT

Born: ANCENIS, FRANCE, 01.03.1993
Signed: JULY 2015
Previous club: NANTES
Debut: BOURNEMOUTH (A) 08.08.2015

WEMBLEY
WONDERLAND!

Villa supporters twice painted Wembley claret and blue in 2015. And even though the FA Cup final was a big disappointment, it was still an occasion to savour as the fans created a magical atmosphere in Wembley's West Stand.

They also occupied that end of the stadium for the semi-final against Liverpool, when Villa recovered from the setback of falling behind to win 2-1 with fabulous goals from Christian Benteke and skipper Fabian Delph.

Many people regarded that afternoon as their best-ever Villa moment. These photos, from both the semi-final and the final, illustrate just how much it means to be at Wembley...

6

CIARAN
CLARK

Tim Sherwood became Villa's 25th manager when he was appointed in February 2015. Here's the lowdown on the boss...

MAY THE FORCE BE WITH YOU!

Timothy Alan Sherwood was born on 6th February 1969 in the village of Elstree, 13 miles north of London. This is the home of Elstree Studios, where some of the world's most famous films – including Star Wars and Indiana Jones – have been made. No wonder they call it Britain's Hollywood!

LITTLE GUNNER BOY

Although he is well known for his time as both player and manager with Tottenham Hotspur, he supported Spurs' north London rivals Arsenal when he was a boy.

A HORNETS' NEST...

The classy midfielder began his professional career with Watford, making his first-team debut for the Hornets against Sheffield Wednesday on 12th September 1987.

TIM OF THE ROVERS

By far the largest period of his playing career was spent with Blackburn Rovers. He made nearly 250 Premier League appearances in seven years at Ewood Park club and helped Rovers to become champions in 1994-95. His other clubs as a player were Norwich City, Tottenham Hotspur, Portsmouth and Coventry City.

INTERNATIONAL HONOURS

He made his England debut at the age of 30 in 1999 in a World Cup qualifier against Poland at Wembley, and made a total of three appearances for the national team. Earlier in his career, he played four times for England under-21s and once for England B.

SCORING AGAINST VILLA

He is the 17th Villa manager to have actually played against the boys in claret and blue – and he had a habit of scoring against Villa. He was on target against us twice for Blackburn and twice for Tottenham.

HARRY'S No 2

His first managerial experience was at White Hart Lane in 2008, when he was appointed assistant to Harry Redknapp. He then became Spurs' technical director before taking charge of the first team in December 2013. His last match as boss was a 3-0 home win against Villa on the final day of the 2013-14 season.

European Adventures

September 2015 marked the 40th anniversary of Villa's first action in European competition – a UEFA Cup-tie against Royal Antwerp in 1975.

Since then, the club have played in more than 20 different countries, in the European Cup, UEFA Cup, Super Cup, Intertoto Cup and Europa League.

This map shows all the destinations for the boys in claret and blue over the course of four decades. And let's not forget all the home legs at Villa Park!

01 BELGIUM
Royal Antwerp 1975
Anderlecht 1982

02 TURKEY
Fenerbahce 1977
Besiktas 1982
Trabzonspor 1994

03 POLAND
Gornik Zabrze 1977

04 SPAIN
Athletic Bilbao 1977, 1997
Barcelona 1978, 1983
Deportivo La Coruna 1993
Atletico Madrid 1998
Celta Vigo 1998, 2000

05 ICELAND (INSET)
Valur 1981
Hafnarfjordur 2008

06 GERMANY
Dynamo Berlin 1981
Hamburg 2008

07 UKRAINE
Dynamo Kiev 1982

08 HOLLAND
Bayern Munich
(European Cup final) 1982

09 ROMANIA
Dinamo Bucharest 1982
Steaua Bucharest 1997

10 ITALY
Juventus 1983
Inter Milan 1990, 1994

11 PORTUGAL
Vitoria Guimaraes 1983

12 RUSSIA
Moscow Spartak 1983
CSKA Moscow 2009

**13 CZECHOSLOVAKIA/
CZECH REPUBLIC**
Banik Ostrava 1990
Marila Pribram 2000
Slavia Prague 2008

14 SLOVAKIA
Slovan Bratislava 1993

15 SWEDEN
Helsingborgs 1996

16 FRANCE
Bordeaux 1997
Stade Rennais 2001
Lille 2002

17 NORWAY
Stromsgodset 1998

18 CROATIA
Slaven Belupo 2001
Varteks 2001

19 SWITZERLAND
Basel 2001
Zurich 2002

20 DENMARK
Odense 2008

21 BULGARIA
Litex Lovech 2008

22 AUSTRIA
Rapid Vienna 2009, 2010

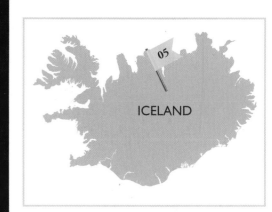

ICELAND

IRELAND

UNITED KINGDOM

FRANCE

PORTUGAL

SPAIN

FINLAND

15 SWEDEN

17 NORWAY

ESTONIA

LATVIA

12 RUSSIA

LITHUANIA

20 DENMARK

BELARUS

08 03 POLAND

HERLANDS

06 GERMANY

01 LGIUM

LUXEMBOURG

07 UKRAINE

13 CZECH REPUBLIC

14 SLOVAKIA

22

19 SWITZERLAND

AUSTRIA

18 HUNGARY

SLOVENIA

MOLDOVA

09 ROMANIA

10 ITALY

CROATIA

BOSNIA AND HERZEGOVINA

SERBIA

21 BULGARIA

MONTENEGRO

KOSOVO

FYRO MACEDONIA

ALBANIA

02

GREECE

TURKEY

SEASON REVIEW

AUGUST

We're off to a flying start! The season opens with a 1-0 win against Stoke City at the Britannia Stadium, where Andi Weimann's right-foot shot secures three points. New signing Philippe Senderos settles in quickly to form a solid central defensive partnership with skipper Ron Vlaar, while midfielder Kieran Richardson and left-back Aly Cissokho also enjoy fine debuts.

That's followed by a goalless draw at home to Newcastle United the following Saturday, and although Paul Lambert's side suffer a shock exit to Leyton Orient in the Capital One Cup, they are soon back to winning ways with a 2-1 success over Hull City.

A fabulous first half display sees Villa go ahead through Gabby Agbonlahor, who swivels to drill a powerful 14th-minute shot into the bottom corner. Then Richardson crosses for Weimann to control with his right foot before firing home with his left from eight yards.

Results

Aug 16	STOKE CITY	A	1-0	Weimann
Aug 23	NEWCASTLE UNITED	H	0-0	
Aug 27	LEYTON ORIENT (C1Cup)	H	0-1	
Aug 31	HULL CITY	H	2-1	Agbonlahor, Weimann

SEPTEMBER

Villa's good record at Liverpool in recent seasons is maintained as Gabby Agbonlahor's Ninth-minute goal makes it two wins and a draw from the last three visits to Anfield.

It also maintains an impressive unbeaten start to the season for the boys in claret and blue, who finish the day second in the table. Villa's possession amounts to just 25 per cent yet they are twice close to scoring in the opening 20 minutes, Philippe Senderos heading over from a good position and Andi Weimann's volley being headed away by Steven Gerrard. The breakthrough arrives when a Senderos header is blocked in a crowded goalmouth, Gabby stabbing home the rebound.

The following week, Villa are hit by a sickness virus which leaves them depleted for the home match against Arsenal. They perform well for half an hour before conceding three goals in the space of four minutes.

Results

Date	Opponent		Score	Scorers
Sept 13	LIVERPOOL	A	1-0	Agbonlahor
Sept 20	ARSENAL	H	0-3	
Sept 27	CHELSEA	A	0-3	

OCTOBER

No goals, no points, very few chances – it really is a month to forget from a claret and blue perspective.

A home defeat by champions Manchester City is heartbreaking because Villa defend so well, with keeper Brad Guzan making some outstanding saves, until the visitors pounce twice in the final eight minutes through Yaya Toure and Sergio Aguero.

But the team are soundly beaten at both Everton and Queens Park Rangers, with the 2-0 defeat at Loftus Road a particularly low point.

Results

Oct 4	MANCHESTER CITY	H	0-2
Oct 18	EVERTON	A	0-3
Oct 27	QUEENS PARK RANGERS	A	0-2

NOVEMBER

Andi Weimann's 16th-minute goal raises hopes of a win at home to Tottenham, the Austrian sliding in front of Younes Kaboul to stab a low shot just inside the near post.

But it's an uphill battle after Christian Benteke is sent off 25 minutes from the end, Spurs hitting back to win 2-1 with goals from Nacer Chadli and Harry Kane.

Some stubborn defending enables Villa to take a point from a goalless draw at West Ham, and the team follow up with two 1-1 draws – at home to Southampton and away to Burnley.

Paul Lambert's side take the lead in both games, Gabby Agbonlahor using his pace to go past 'Saints' 'keeper' Fraser Forster while Joe Cole's clever near-post conversion gives the former Chelsea player his first Villa goal.

Results

Nov 2	TOTTENHAM HOTSPUR	H	1-2	Weimann
Nov 8	WEST HAM	A	0-0	
Nov 24	SOUTHAMPTON	H	1-1	Agbonlahor
Nov 29	BURNLEY	A	1-1	Cole

DECEMBER

Christian Benteke secures victory over Crystal Palace with a magnificent curling shot at Selhurst Park, and a few days later Villa make it back-to-back wins by beating Leicester City at home.

After Leandro Ulloa puts the Foxes ahead, Villa draw level when defender Ciaran Clark launches himself to flick home a superb header from Ashley Westwood's free-kick. Right-back Alan Hutton hits the winner with a low shot inside the near post after controlling Benteke's excellent diagonal pass.

Kieran Richardson is sent off against West Brom, who take the points with a goal from former Villan Craig Gardner.

Another stunning Benteke goal gives Villa the lead against Manchester United, but the visitors hit back with a headed equaliser from Radamel Falcao.

Results

Dec 2	CRYSTAL PALACE	A	1-0	Benteke
Dec 7	LEICESTER CITY	H	2-1	Clark, Hutton
Dec 13	WEST BROMWICH ALBION	A	0-1	
Dec 20	MANCHESTER UNITED	H	1-1	Benteke
Dec 26	SWANSEA CITY	A	0-1	
Dec 28	SUNDERLAND	H	0-0	

JANUARY

Up for the Cup! Villa's league form continues to be disappointing, their only point in January coming from a goalless draw at home to Crystal Palace. But they make progress in the FA Cup against two of the country's seaside teams.

Blackpool, struggling at the bottom of the Championship, arrive at Villa Park on the first weekend of the year and give us a real scare, keeper Shay Given twice having to make important saves. Just as a replay is looming, Christian Benteke controls the ball on the edge of the penalty area before drilling home an unstoppable right-foot volley.

Next up, it's Championship leaders Bournemouth and the fourth-round tie is a triumph for Villa's new Spanish signing Carles Gil, who opens the scoring with a sensational first goal for the club before Andi Weimann doubles the lead with a less spectacular but superbly constructed effort.

Results

Jan 1	CRYSTAL PALACE	H	0-0	
Jan 4	BLACKPOOL (FA Cup 3)	H	1-0	Benteke
Jan 10	LEICESTER CITY	A	0-1	
Jan 17	LIVERPOOL	H	0-2	
Jan 25	BOURNEMOUTH (FA Cup 4)	H	2-1	Gil, Weimann

FEBRUARY

The FA Cup provides the high spot, Villa beating Leicester City 2-1 with a rising shot from Leandro Bacuna and a late effort from Scott Sinclair, who has signed on loan from Manchester City. Sinclair's shot is initially saved by Mark Schwarzer but the Foxes keeper then fumbles the ball over the line.

The match is watched by new manager Tim Sherwood, who has just been appointed following the departure of Paul Lambert.

On the league front, unfortunately, it's a dismal month. Jores Okore scores his first goal for the club in the home match against Chelsea while Sinclair follows up his Cup strike by heading the team ahead against Stoke City – but by the end of the month Villa have suffered seven consecutive Premier League setbacks and are in the relegation zone.

Results

Feb 1	ARSENAL	A	0-5	
Feb 7	CHELSEA	H	1-2	Okore
Feb 10	HULL CITY	A	0-2	
Feb 15	LEICESTER CITY (FA Cup 5)	H	2-1	Bacuna, Sinclair
Feb 21	STOKE CITY	H	1-2	Sinclair
Feb 28	NEWCASTLE UNITED	A	0-1	

MARCH

Results

Mar 3	WEST BROM	H	2-1	Agbonlahor, Benteke pen
Mar 7	WEST BROM (FA Cup 6)	H	2-0	Delph, Sinclair
Mar 14	SUNDERLAND	A	4-0	Benteke 2, Agbonlahor 2
Mar 21	SWANSEA CITY	H	0-1	

Tim Sherwood's men beat West Brom twice in the space of five days.

First up is a Barclays Premier League match, and the home side lead at half-time through Gabby Agbonlahor's low drive after Christian Benteke heads on Brad Guzan's long kick downfield.

Saido Berahino heads a 66th-minute equaliser, but stoppage time brings high drama. Ben Foster brings down Matt Lowton, and from the resultant penalty Benteke cheekily tricks the keeper into diving the wrong way.

In the FA Cup the following Saturday, Charles N'Zogbia sets up acting captain Fabian Delph for the opening goal and five minutes from the end Scott Sinclair moves on to Jack Grealish's pass to curl a shot past Ben Foster.

Villa are in rampant mood at the Stadium of Light, tearing Sunderland apart in the first half with two goals each for Benteke and Agbonlahor.

APRIL

Results

April 4	MANCHESTER UNITED	A	1-3	Benteke	
April 7	QUEENS PARK RANGERS	H	3-3	Benteke 3	
April 11	TOTTENHAM HOTSPUR	A	1-0	Benteke	
April 19	LIVERPOOL (FA Cup s/f)	W	2-1	Benteke, Delph	
April 25	MANCHESTER CITY	A	2-3	Sanchez, Cleverley	

After a not unexpected defeat at Manchester United, Christian Benteke's hat-trick earns a 3-3 home draw against Queens Park Rangers, with Villa trailing 1-0, leading 2-1 and trailing 3-2 before the Belgian striker's free-kick earns a point.

It's Benteke's second Premier League hat-trick, and he follows up with the only goal in a 1-0 success over Sherwood's former club Tottenham Hotspur at White Hart Lane.

At the end of the month, Tom Cleverley and Carlos Sanchez both score their first Villa goals as Tim Sherwood's team slip to an unlucky 3-2 defeat by Manchester City.

But the real highlight of April is a sensational FA Cup semi-final victory over Liverpool. On a glorious afternoon at Wembley, Benteke claims his ninth goal in seven games to cancel out Philippe Coutinho's opener for the Merseysiders before skipper Fabian Delph hits a second-half winner.

Safe at last! Two consecutive home games offer Villa the opportunity to amass some valuable points and they grab the opportunity with both hands, beating both Everton and West Ham.

Christian Benteke opens the scoring against the Toffees, climbing to meet Fabian Delph's 10th-minute cross with a header past keeper Tim Howard. And the Belgium international is on target again on 39 minutes, driving the ball into the roof of the net following a Jack Grealish corner.

Although Romelu Lukaku reduces the deficit in the second half, Tom Cleverley effectively secures three points by moving on to Leandro Bacuna's perfect through ball to drive into the roof of the net.

A week later, Cleverley makes it three goals in three games with the winner against the Hammers, side-footing home from five yards following some tricky footwork and a fine low cross from Grealish.

Premier League safety is guaranteed, ironically, on a day when Villa endure a nightmare at St Mary's, crashing 6-1 to Southampton. It's an afternoon to forget on the south coast but on the journey home the players learn that Hull City have lost at Tottenham, which means Villa are staying in the top flight.

Our FA Cup dreams, sadly, are ended by a 4-0 defeat at the hands of Arsenal in the final at Wembley.

Results

Date	Opponent		Score	Scorers
May 2	EVERTON	H	3-2	Benteke 2, Cleverley
May 9	WEST HAM	H	1-0	Cleverley
May 16	SOUTHAMPTON	A	1-6	Benteke
May 24	BURNLEY	H	0-1	
May 30	ARSENAL (FA Cup final)	W	0-4	

★ ★ ★ ★ ★ ★ ★ ★ ★ ★ ★ ★ ★ ★ ★

FINAL BARCLAYS PREMIER LEAGUE TABLE

Pos	Team	P	W	D	L	F	A	GD	Pts
1	Chelsea	38	26	9	3	73	32	41	87
2	Manchester City	38	24	7	7	83	38	45	79
3	Arsenal	38	22	9	7	71	36	35	75
4	Manchester United	38	20	10	8	62	37	25	70
5	Tottenham Hotspur	38	19	7	12	58	53	5	64
6	Liverpool	38	18	8	12	52	48	4	62
7	Southampton	38	18	6	14	54	33	21	60
8	Swansea City	38	16	8	14	46	49	-3	56
9	Stoke City	38	15	9	14	48	45	3	54
10	Crystal Palace	38	13	9	16	47	51	-4	48
11	Everton	38	12	11	15	48	50	-2	47
12	West Ham United	38	12	11	15	44	47	-3	47
13	West Bromwich Albion	38	11	11	16	38	51	-13	44
14	Leicester City	38	11	8	19	46	55	-9	41
15	Newcastle United	38	10	9	19	40	63	-23	39
16	Sunderland	38	7	17	14	31	53	-22	38
17	ASTON VILLA	38	10	8	20	31	57	-26	38
18	Hull City	38	8	11	19	33	51	-18	35
19	Burnley	38	7	12	19	28	53	-25	33
20	Queens Park Rangers	38	8	6	24	42	73	-31	30

APPEARANCES AND SCORERS

1 BRAD GUZAN
A 34 league

2 NATHAN BAKER
A 8(3) league, 2 cup

4 RON VLAAR
A 19(1) league, 3 cup

5 JORES OKORE
A 22(1) league, 4(1) cup
G 1 league

6 CIARAN CLARK
A 22(3) league, 4 cup
G 1 league

7 LEANDRO BACUNA
A 10(9) league, 5(2) cup
G 1 cup

8 TOM CLEVERLEY
A 31 league, 6 cup
G 3 league

9 SCOTT SINCLAIR
A 5(4) league, 1(2) cup
G 1 league, 2 cup

10 ANDREAS WEIMANN
A 20(11) league, 2(2) cup
G 3 league, 1 cup

11 GABRIEL AGBONLAHOR
A 30(4) league, 1(1) cup
G 6 league

12 JOE COLE
A 3(9) league, 2(1) cup
G 1 league

13 JED STEER
A 1 league

14 PHILIPPE SENDEROS
A 7(1) league, 1 cup

15 ASHLEY WESTWOOD
A 25(2) league, 6(1) cup

16 FABIAN DELPH
A 27(1) league, 4 cup
G 2 cup

18 KIERAN RICHARDSON
A 16 (6) league, 4 cup

19 DARREN BENT
A 0(7) league, 1 cup

20 CHRISTIAN BENTEKE
A 26(3) league, 5 cup
G 13 league, 2 cup

21 ALAN HUTTON
A 27(3) league, 5 cup
G 1 league

23 ALY CISSOKHO
A 24(1) league, 2 cup

24 CARLOS SANCHEZ
A 20(8) league, 3(2) cup
G 1 league

25 CARLES GIL
A 4(1) league, 1(1) cup
G 1 cup

28 CHARLES N'ZOGBIA
A 19(8) league, 3(1) cup

29 RUSHIAN HEPBURN-MURPHY
A 0(1) league

31 SHAY GIVEN
A 3 league, 7 cup

34 MATT LOWTON
A 8(4) league, 1 cup

40 JACK GREALISH
A 7(10) league, 4(3) cup

KEY:

A APPEARANCES
G GOALS

CUP FINAL

Villa reached the FA Cup final for the 11th time last season, although they have faced only eight other clubs in English football's showpiece game. That's because our first three finals were all against West Bromwich Albion (1887, 1892 and 1895) and we also played Newcastle United in both 1905 and 1924.

Our other finals have been against Everton (1897), Sunderland (1913), Huddersfield Town (1920), Manchester United (1957), Chelsea (2000) and, of course, Arsenal in 2015.

We have hidden the eight clubs – plus Villa – in this Cup Final word search. Can you find them? These are the names you are looking for:

HUDDERSFIELD	SUNDERLAND
NEWCASTLE	MAN UNITED
ARSENAL	CHELSEA
EVERTON	WEST BROM
VILLA	

```
H A N E W C A S T L E B
C U W E S T B R O M V F
E G D K M O R M E D E X
I Q U D T A P H M N R P
S U N D E R L A N D T Q
L C V I K R O S K N O R
F H J W X T S T L Z N S
B E Y D E R C F M E X J
D L G U M B Q V I L L A
V S A R S E N A L E S C
N E H Y F C L J D D L I
P A B M A N U N I T E D
```

ANSWERS ON PAGE 61

1

BRADLEY
GUZAN

Whose shirt is it?

Someone has mixed up all the letters while putting Villa's players' names on the back of their shirts. Can you unravel the letters to reveal the correct name on each shirt?

ROOK E
1

....

LACK R
2

....

ILEG RASH
3

....

CARL IS IN
4

....

HOBO RAN GAL
5

....

BREAK
6

....

ZEN CASH
7

....

CRASH RID
8

....

SID OR RANCH
9

....

SOW TO WED
10

....

CARL GILES
11

....

A NAG
12

....

Great Scots!

Crossword grid with vertical answer: A L A N H U T T O N

1. Andy G - All-action striker who was a true Holte End hero.
2. Alex C - Skilful midfielder whose career was ended by a serious injury.
3. Allan E - Originally a striker, he became a dependable central defender, helping Villa to European Cup glory.
4. Alan M - Striker who scored crucial goals before joining Bayern Munich in 1989.
5. Ray H - This midfielder played for the Republic of Ireland but was born in Glasgow.
6. Ken M - Central defender who was in Villa's League Championship and European Cup-winning teams.
7. Stiliyan P - Not a Scot, but he signed from Celtic!
8. Charlie A - Left-back who made a record 660 appearances for the club.
9. Bobby T - An inside-forward who scored lots of goals in the late 1950s and early 1960s.
10. Barry B - Talented youngster who didn't quite realise his full potential before moving to Crystal Palace.

ANSWERS ON PAGE 61

Do you know
Brad Guzan?

01
GK

 In which American city, popularly known as the "Windy City" was Brad born?

ANSWER:

- -

2 From which club did Brad join Villa in 2008 – Chicago Fire, Chivas USA or LA Galaxy?

ANSWER:

- -

3 In a League Cup tie in 2009, Brad saved a spot kick during the match and then another three during the penalty shoot-out. Which team did Villa beat to reach the quarter-finals?

ANSWER:

- -

4 He was understudy to two other top keepers – an American and an Irishman – before becoming Villa's first-choice. Can you name them?

ANSWER:

- -

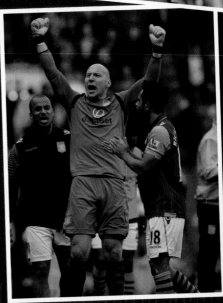

5 Can you remember which club Brad joined on loan in 2011?

ANSWER:

- -

ANSWERS ON PAGE 60

40

JACK GREALISH

The Supermacs!

Prolific striker Malcolm Macdonald was the original "Supermac" during his days with Newcastle United in the 1970s, but Villa have also had a few Supermacs down the years. Can you name these five?

Funny Faces

We have mixed up a few players' head shots, creating some funny faces. Can you tell whose hair, eyes and chins are pictured?

1

Hair:

Eyes:

Chin:

2

Hair:

Eyes:

Chin:

3

Hair:

Eyes:

Chin:

8

IDRISSA **GANA**

Guess who?

CAN YOU REVEAL THE IDENTITY OF SIX VILLA PLAYERS FROM THE CLUES BELOW?
If you can answer after clue A, you receive three points. If you're right after clue B, award yourself two points, and if you need to use clue C you get one point. And if the player's name still escapes you, check the answers at the back of the Annual!

A
1. I WAS BORN IN ENGLAND BUT I HAVE PLAYED INTERNATIONAL FOOTBALL FOR THE REPUBLIC OF IRELAND.
2. I MADE MY VILLA DEBUT AGAINST FULHAM IN 2009.
3. ALTHOUGH I'M A DEFENDER I ONCE SCORED TWO GOALS AGAINST ARSENAL – AND WE STILL LOST 4-2.

B
1. I SIGNED FOR VILLA FROM AN ITALIAN CLUB.
2. I DIDN'T PLAY A SINGLE FIRST-TEAM MATCH LAST SEASON BECAUSE OF A SERIOUS INJURY.
3. I'M A STRIKER AND I WAS BORN IN THE CZECH REPUBLIC.

C
1. I SIGNED FOR VILLA THIS SUMMER.
2. I'M A DEFENSIVE MIDFIELDER.
3. I WAS BORN IN SENEGAL BUT HAVE SPENT MOST OF MY CAREER IN FRANCE.

D
1. I WAS BORN IN BIRMINGHAM AND GREW UP AS A VILLA SUPPORTER.
2. I'M A MIDFIELDER AND I MADE MY DEBUT AT MANCHESTER CITY IN MAY 2014.
3. I HAVE TWICE BEEN VILLA'S LEADING SCORER IN THE HONG KONG SEVENS TOURNAMENT.

E
1. I'VE HAD A FEW LOAN SPELLS DURING MY TIME WITH VILLA – INCLUDING ONE WITH SPANISH CLUB REAL MALLORCA.
2. I JOINED THE CLUB FROM TOTTENHAM HOTSPUR.
3. I WAS BORN IN GLASGOW AND I'M A SCOTLAND INTERNATIONAL.

F
1. I MADE MY VILLA DEBUT IN A 1-0 WIN AT STOKE CITY ON THE OPENING DAY OF LAST SEASON.
2. I WAS BORN IN THE GREENWICH AREA OF LONDON.
3. MY PREVIOUS CLUBS INCLUDE MANCHESTER UNITED, SUNDERLAND AND FULHAM.

ANSWERS ON PAGE 60

11

GABRIEL **AGBONLAHOR**

CAN WE PLAY YOU EVERY SEASON?

COVER STORY

Throughout the 2014-15 season, Villa produced programme covers based on designs from previous seasons. And for the historic 200th league game against Everton in May, we went right back to 1948-49, when the Villa News & Record featured a colour cover for the first time.

Aston Villa v Everton is more than a football match – it is the most-played league fixture in the country.

The clubs first met in competitive action when they were among the 12 founder members of the Football League in 1888, Villa winning 2-1 with two goals from Dennis Hodgetts.

When they faced each other at Villa Park in May 2015, it was the 200th league fixture between the clubs. And every one of those games was played in English football's top flight – either the old First Division or, since 1992, the Premier League.

At the end of last season, the Merseyside club held a slight advantage, with a total of 74 wins to Villa's 73, the other 53 games having ended as draws.

Needless to say, there have been some classic contests down the years, none more dramatic than Villa's 3-2 win at Goodison Park in 2008 when Joleon Lescott scored the Toffees' second equaliser in stoppage time before Ashley Young went straight to the other end and hit Villa's winner.

The game in May was also crucial, because Villa were under threat of relegation. But another 3-2 victory helped the boy in claret and blue to stay in the top division.

Here's to another 200 Villa-Everton league games!

Villa didn't have a programme until 1906 but Everton produced this pocket-sized edition for the second league game between the clubs

SPOT THE
DIFFERENCE

Spot the five differences between these two photographs.
Turn to page 60 to see if you are spot on!

WHERE IT ALL STARTED

These players all proudly wear the claret and blue of Aston Villa. But we've mixed up the clubs for whom they made their professional debuts. Match up the players' names with the correct clubs and check out the answers on page 61.

MICAH RICHARDS

SCOTT SINCLAIR

JORES OKORE

KIERAN RICHARDSON

ALAN HUTTON

Crewe Alexandra

Nice

Nordsjaelland

Aston Villa

Manchester City

Bristol Rovers

Slezsky Opava

River Plate Montevideo

Manchester United

Glasgow Rangers

ASHLEY WESTWOOD

JORDAN AMAVI

LIBOR KOZAK

CIARAN CLARK

CARLOS SANCHEZ

9

SCOTT
SINCLAIR

ACCESS ALL AREAS

Hercules has an "access all areas" pass to Villa Park, and has been prowling into areas that the public never see.
But our lovable lion can't recall which rooms he has visited. Can you help him out by matching this list with the photos of the places he has been?
To get you started, number 1 is the TV Studio. See how many others you can identify. Check out the answers on page 61.

VIP ACCESS
★ ★ ★

TV STUDIO
ARCHIVE ROOM
FIRST AID ROOM
KITCHENS
LEARNING CENTRE
PITCH MAINTENANCE AREA
PRESS CONFERENCE ROOM
STADIUM CONTROL ROOM
VILLA STORE WAREHOUSE
POLICE CELLS

1: Tv Studio

2:

3:

4:

5:

6:

7:

8:

9:

10:

STRANGE BUT TRUE!

Well done young Brown!

Jimmy Brown created a Villa record that is unlikely to be broken when he made his debut away to Bolton Wanderers in September 1969. Brown was just 15 years and 349 days old, making him the youngest player ever to represent Villa in a first team fixture.

Villa's youngest first-team scorer was Walter Hazelden, who was 16 when he netted on his debut in a 3-2 defeat by West Bromwich Albion at The Hawthorns in November 1957.

A 'dream' goal

Footballers often refer to winning the FA Cup as "a dream come true". And although it's just a figure of speech, it actually happened to Clem Stephenson.

On the night before the 1913 final, the Villa forward dreamt his team would beat Sunderland with a headed goal from Tommy Barber.

He even told Sunderland player Charlie Buchan before kick-off – and 11 minutes from the end, Barber headed the winner!

The super subs

Substitutes are part and parcel of modern day football, with managers able to use three of the seven subs at their disposal. But until the mid-sixties, substitutes simply did not exist. If a player had to go off injured, it was just bad luck.

But things changed at the start of the 1965-66 season when all Football League teams were allowed one sub. Graham Parker became Villa's first sub when he replaced Tony Hateley in the match at home to Tottenham in September 1965.

The first Villa sub to score a goal was Lew Chatterley (pictured) who was on target after replacing Mike Tindall in a 3-2 home victory over Blackpool in January 1967.

Played none, scored one!

Which Villa player scored for the club without ever playing for the club? It's a trick question, of course. Czech Republic midfielder Ivo Stas wasn't wearing a Villa shirt when he scored for us. He conceded an own goal while playing against us for Banik Ostrava in the UEFA Cup in 1990. Shortly afterwards he signed for Villa but never played in a competitive game because of injury.

23

JORDAN **AMAVI**

It's a fact!

Every season tends to throw up some fascinating facts and figures, and the 2014-15 campaign was no different...

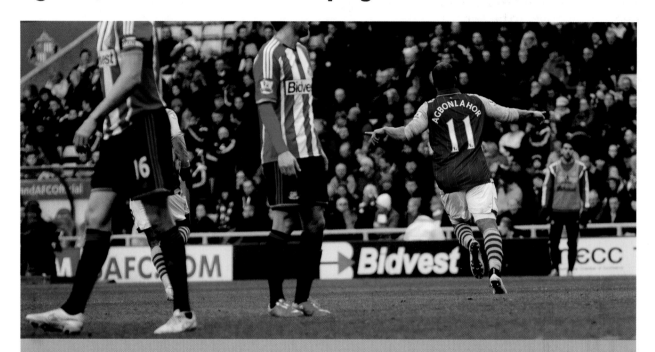

300-up for Gabby

Gabby Agbonlahor has already established himself as the club's leading Premier League scorer, passing the record previously held by Dwight Yorke. Now he has his sights set on playing more Premier League games than any other Villa player.

Gabby made his 300th Premier League appearance in the 4-0 win at Sunderland in March, when he also added two more goals to his total. His next target is to pass the 365 Premier appearances made by Gareth Barry between 1998 and 2009.

A double century...

Carles Gil made a small piece of Villa history when he made his debut in the home match against Chelsea in February.

The Spanish midfielder became the 200th player to represent the club in the Premier League since its formation in 1992.

Four in 45...

Villa scored just four goals in the first 14 away matches – and then doubled their total with four in 45 minutes at Sunderland!

Christian Benteke and Gabby Agbonlahor were both on target twice in the first-half romp at the Stadium of Light.

The previous four away goals had all been productive, to be fair, yielding 1-0 wins at Stoke City, Liverpool and Crystal Palace, plus a 1-1 draw at Burnley.

Luck of the draw

Villa were drawn at home in every round of the FA Cup, beating Blackpool, Bournemouth, Leicester City and West Bromwich Albion en route to a Wembley semi-final against Liverpool.

It was only the fourth time the club had been handed home draws all the way to the semi-final, the other occasions being 1887, 1985 and 1905. And the sixth-round game against Albion was Villa's first home quarter-final for 55 years!

The trend even continued at Wembley, where Villa won the toss to wear their home kit and occupy the "home" dressing room for both the semi-final against Liverpool and the final against Arsenal.

If you're good enough...

Rushian Hepburn-Murphy became Villa's youngest Premier League player when he went on as an 83rd-minute substitute in the 4-0 victory at Sunderland in March.

The Birmingham-born striker was 16 years and 176 days old on the day he made his debut, beating the record previously held by Gareth Barry, who was 17 when he played his first Premier League game in 1998.

Hepburn-Murphy also became the third-youngest player in Villa's history, after Jimmy Brown (15 years and 349 days) and Norman Ashe (16 years and 48 days).

As the old saying goes, if you're good enough, you're old enough!

2014-15 Debuts

ALY CISSOKHO v STOKE CITY (A)

PHILIPPE SENDEROS v STOKE CITY (A)

KIERAN RICHARDSON v STOKE CITY (A)

CARLOS SANCHEZ v NEWCASTLE UNITED (H)

JOE COLE v LEYTON ORIENT (H)

TOM CLEVERLEY v LIVERPOOL (A)

CARLES GIL v LIVERPOOL (H)

SCOTT SINCLAIR v ARSENAL (A)

RUSHIAN HEPBURN-MURPHY v SUNDERLAND (A)

BRIGHTER THAN EVER!

JV-Life membership is the best way for young supporters to keep in touch with what's happening to their favourite players. A fantastic free magazine is sent out four times a year to every member of Villa's junior club for youngsters aged 14 and under.

And the magazine is now brighter and better than ever. You will find colour photos and interviews with Villa's star players, plus puzzles, comic strips, jokes, competitions and lots more fun-filled pages, all aimed especially at younger supporters.

The magazine is just one of the benefits you will receive as a full member of the club. New members receive the following items in their welcome pack:
• Welcome letter from Hercules
• An official JV-Life certificate
• Exclusive JV-Life snood, plus a set of three button badges
• A membership card
• JV-Life magazine four times a year

Members also receive a birthday card and Christmas card, plus invites to exclusive JV-Life parties where there's often a chance to meet some of Villa's players. Last year we visited the National Sea Life Centre with Jack Grealish, Carlos Sanchez and Callum Robinson!

Your membership card also entitles you to certain discounts around the club including a free place on our Kickin' Kids Parties plus a free stadium tour.

ONLY 19.95 A YEAR

FREE MEMBERSHIP FOR JUNIOR SEASON TICKET HOLDERS

BENEFITS INCLUDE:

The chance to become a matchday mascot
£1 ticket offers
Exclusive events and competitions
PLUS SO MUCH MORE!

SO YOU WANT TO BE A MASCOT?

Being a full member of JV-Life means you will have the chance to be a matchday mascot, which is an unforgettable experience for any young supporter.

Get a taste for the amazing atmosphere of walking out at Villa Park as a mascot by watching our Mascot Cam from the Villa v West Brom game last season. Search for 'AVFC mascot cam' on YouTube!

If you are lucky enough to be randomly selected, you will get the chance to display your skills on the pitch before kick-off, sit in the home dug-out, walk out with the players and lineup for the handshakes with the opposition. You will also receive a souvenir photo of your big day.

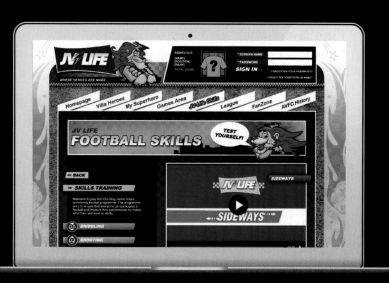

FUNANDGAMESONLINE >> www.jvlife.co.uk

Apart from the full membership package, a free online JV-Life lite membership is available to all Villa fans aged 14 and under.
Sign up online and you will be able to play great games, build your own hero to compete in the JV-Life Super League and learn about living a healthy lifestyle.

It's a *date!*

HOW WELL DO YOU KNOW YOUR CLARET AND BLUE HISTORY?
SEE IF YOU CAN PINPOINT THE YEAR WHEN THESE SIGNIFICANT
EVENTS HAPPENED...CHECK OUT YOUR ANSWERS ON PAGE 61

1. Villa first won the FA Cup in which year?
A 1874 **B** 1887 **C** 1895

2. When did we become Football League champions for the first time?
A 1894 **B** 1897 **C** 1910

3. In which season did Villa score a record 128 league goals but still had to settle for runners-up spot behind Arsenal?
A 1921-22 **B** 1929-30 **C** 1930-31

4. When did Villa play their first European Cup tie?
A 1977 **B** 1981 **C** 1983

5. In what year did Villa and Everton play each other for the 200th time in a league fixture?
A 2013 **B** 2014 **C** 2015

6. Villa faced Chelsea in the last FA Cup final at the old Wembley Stadium. In which year?
A 1998 **B** 2000 **C** 2001

Spot the ball

CAN YOU HELP HERCULES FIND THE BALL IN THIS PICTURE OF MICAH RICHARDS? TURN TO PAGE 60 TO SEE IF YOU ARE RIGHT.

19

JORDAN **AYEW**

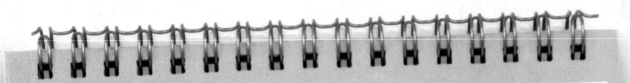

VILLA POPS!

Serves 8
Takes 30 minutes
Ready after an hour
Get an adult to help

What you will need

- **200g white or milk chocolate**
- **A mixture of small claret and blue sweets to decorate – jelly sweets, flowers, butterflies, stars, hundreds and thousands etc**
- **8 lollipop sticks**
- **3 metres of ribbon – claret and blue**
- **2 sheets of greaseproof paper**

What to do

1. Spread the two sheets of greaseproof paper out on a tray. Take a large spoon – a wooden one is best. With a pencil, draw around the spoon, leaving space around each one, and space for the lolly sticks. This will give you eight egg shapes.

2. Break the chocolate into squares, and put it into a heatproof bowl ready for melting. Sit the bowl on top of a pan of gently simmering water, and gently stir the chocolate until it is all melted. (Ask an adult to help you with steps 2 and 3).

3. Take the bowl off the pan, and carry it over to the paper. With a teaspoon, pour a little chocolate out and spread it onto the shapes with the back of the spoon, so that they are all filled with a layer of chocolate. (If the chocolate in the bowl goes hard, put it back over the hot water).

4. Place a lolly stick into each of the chocolate eggs, to make a lollipop. You might need to move the sticks around a bit to make sure that they are covered with chocolate at the top, and are fixed.

5. While the chocolate is still soft, sprinkle the claret and blue sweets all over the top, or make your designs on each lolly.

6. Place the tray in the fridge or a really cool place for an hour, until the lollies are hard. Then gently peel them off the paper, and tie the ribbon around the sticks.

enjoy!

39

RUDY GESTEDE

ANSWERS

SPOT THE DIFFERENCE P 45

SPOT THE BALL P 56

DO YOU KNOW BRAD GUZAN? P 38

1 - CHICAGO
2 - CHIVAS USA
3 - SUNDERLAND
4 - BRAD FRIEDEL AND SHAY GIVEN
5 - HULL CITY

THE SUPERMACS P 40

1 - PAUL McGRATH
2 - ALAN McINALLY
3 - KEN McNAUGHT
4 - PETER McPARLAND
5 - GAVIN McCANN

FUNNY FACES P 40

1 - JACK GREALISH HAIR
  - SHAY GIVEN'S EYES
  - NATHAN BAKER'S CHIN

2 - SHAY GIVEN'S HAIR
  - CHARLES N'ZOGBIA'S EYES
  - JOE COLE'S CHIN

3 - GABBY AGBONLAHOR'S HAIR
  - JORES OKORE'S EYES
  - LEANDRO BACUNA'S CHIN

GUESS WHO? P 42

A - CIARAN CLARK
B - LIBOR KOZAK
C - IDRISSA GUEYE
D - JACK GREALISH
E - ALAN HUTTON
F - KIERAN RICHARDSON

CUP FINAL WORD SEARCH P 34

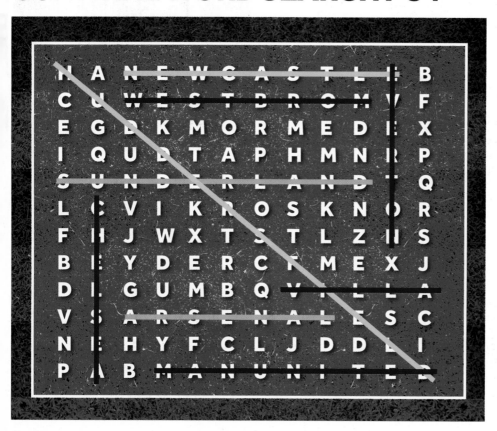

WHERE IT ALL STARTED P 46

1. MICAH RICHARDS (MANCHESTER CITY)
2. SCOTT SINCLAIR (BRISTOL ROVERS)
3. JORES OKORE (NORDSJAELLAND)
4. KIERAN RICHARDSON (MANCHESTER UNITED)
5. ALAN HUTTON (GLASGOW RANGERS)
6. ASHLEY WESTWOOD (CREWE ALEXANDRA)
7. JORDAN AMAVI (NICE)
8. LIBOR KOZAK (SLEZSKY OPAVA)
9. CIARAN CLARK (ASTON VILLA)
10. CARLOS SANCHEZ
(RIVER PLATE MONTEVIDEO)

ACCESS ALL AREAS P 48

1 - TV STUDIO
2 - FIRST AID ROOM
3 - VILLA STORE WAREHOUSE
4 - KITCHENS
5 - STADIUM CONTROL ROOM
6 - LEARNING CENTRE
7 - PRESS CONFERENCE ROOM
8 - POLICE CELLS
9 - ARCHIVE ROOM
10 - PITCH MAINTENANCE AREA

GREAT SCOTS! P 37